Good Morning, Morning, Sunshine

by

Dr. Matt Glowiak

To order additional copies of this book, contact:
Xlibris
844-714-8691
www.Xlibris.com
Orders@Xlibris.com

Library of Congress Control Number: 2022918247
ISBN: Softcover   978-1-6698-3986-6
         Hardcover   978-1-6698-5020-5
         EBook   978-1-6698-3985-9

Print information available on the last page

Rev. date: 09/29/2022

Good morning, sunshine.
Welcome new day.
Rested and ready,
Let's get up and play.

Eyes wide awake—
Not a care in the world,
A fun day lies ahead
Of this I am sure.

After some breakfast
We'll take out your toys
But just one at a time—
The ones you enjoy.

Once toy time is over
We'll go take a walk,
Come home and draw pictures
On the driveway with chalk.

We'll run through the lawn
And blow bubbles for hours,
While naming the colors
We see on the flowers.

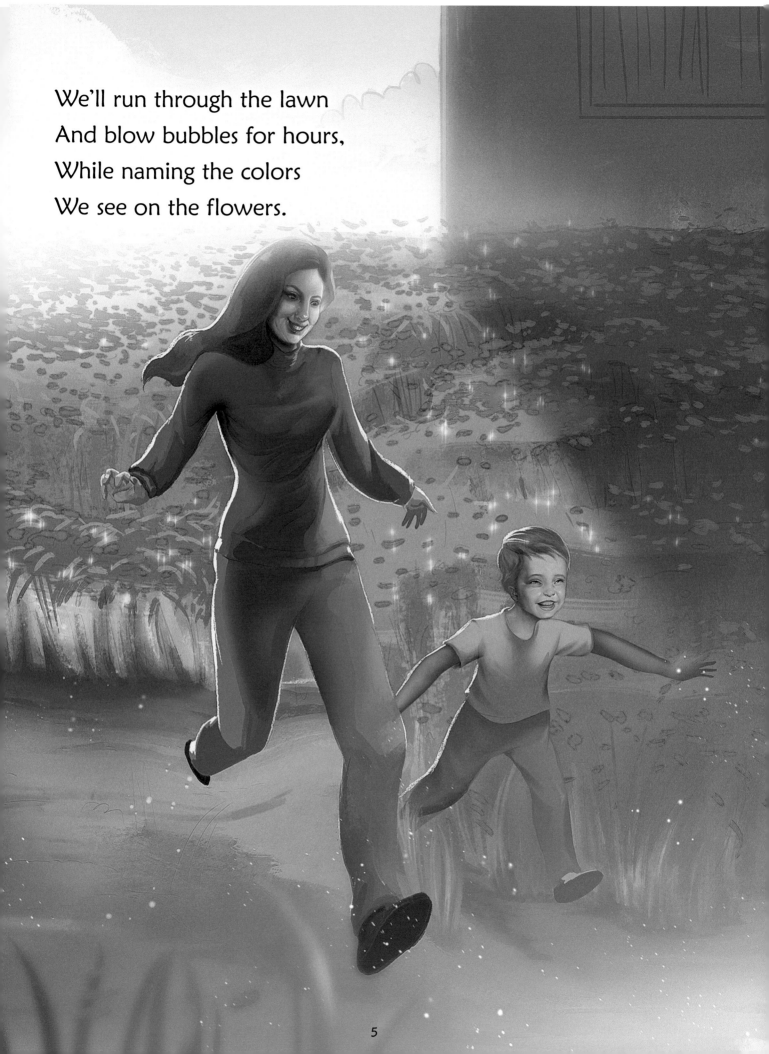

Time has flown by
Now it's time to eat lunch—
With your favorite meal ready,
You'll love it a bunch.

Ring goes the doorbell.
Your best friend's outside.
We'll run around for a while,
Then take your trikes for a ride.

We'll play at the park,
Fly so high on the swings,
Go down every slide,
And climb everything!

We had fun for a while.
Now it's time for goodbye.
You can both play tomorrow,
So please do not cry.

We're both getting tired.
It's okay we can nap.
Snuggled closely and warmly
In your blankie both wrapped.

Rested and ready
We wake up anew
With more time to have fun
So, here's what we'll do!

We'll count all the numbers
On our fingers and toes
And make funny faces
Ready! Set! Go!

Then we'll sing letters
From A all through Z.
I'm so proud of you, baby.
I hope that you see.

Now's time for dinner,
Yes, you must eat your veggies.
With a healthy meal eaten
We'll all fill our bellies

Good evening, moon
Brightly shining above
Alongside the stars
In the space that we love.

Now it's bath time
With bubbles and ducky,
Scrub you all clean
So you're no longer muddy.

Brush all those teeth
From bottom to top
And put on your PJs
Into bed, now hop-hop.

But don't close your eyes yet,
I'll read you a story,
And do all the voices;
We both will laugh surely.

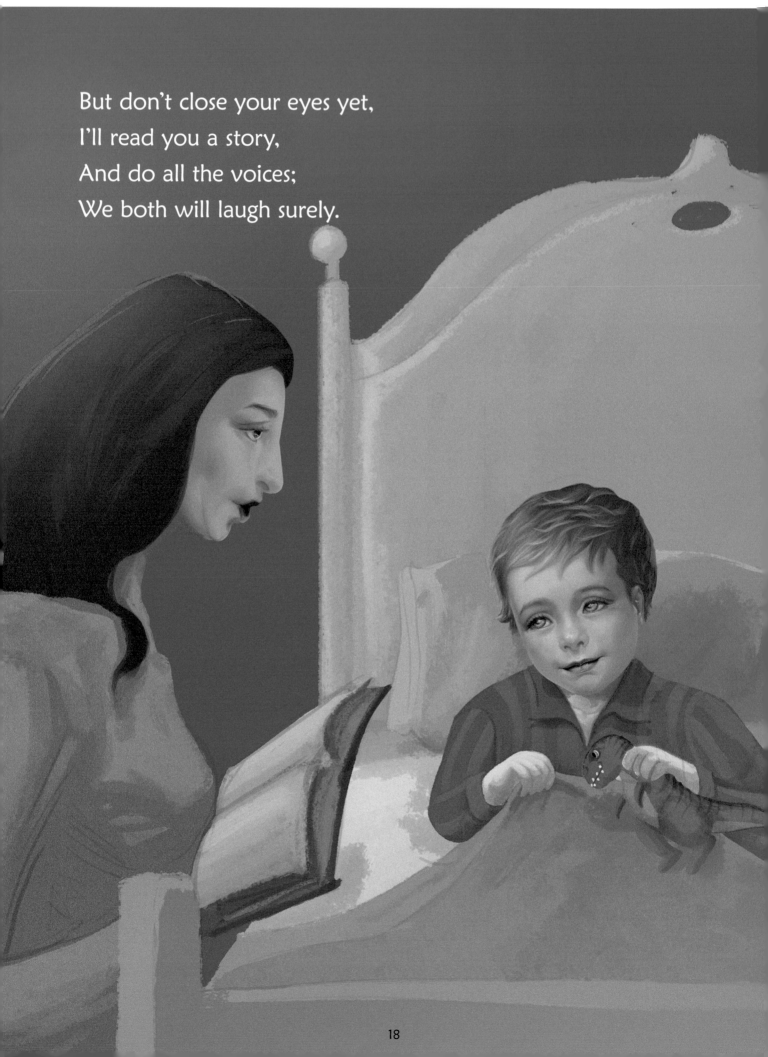

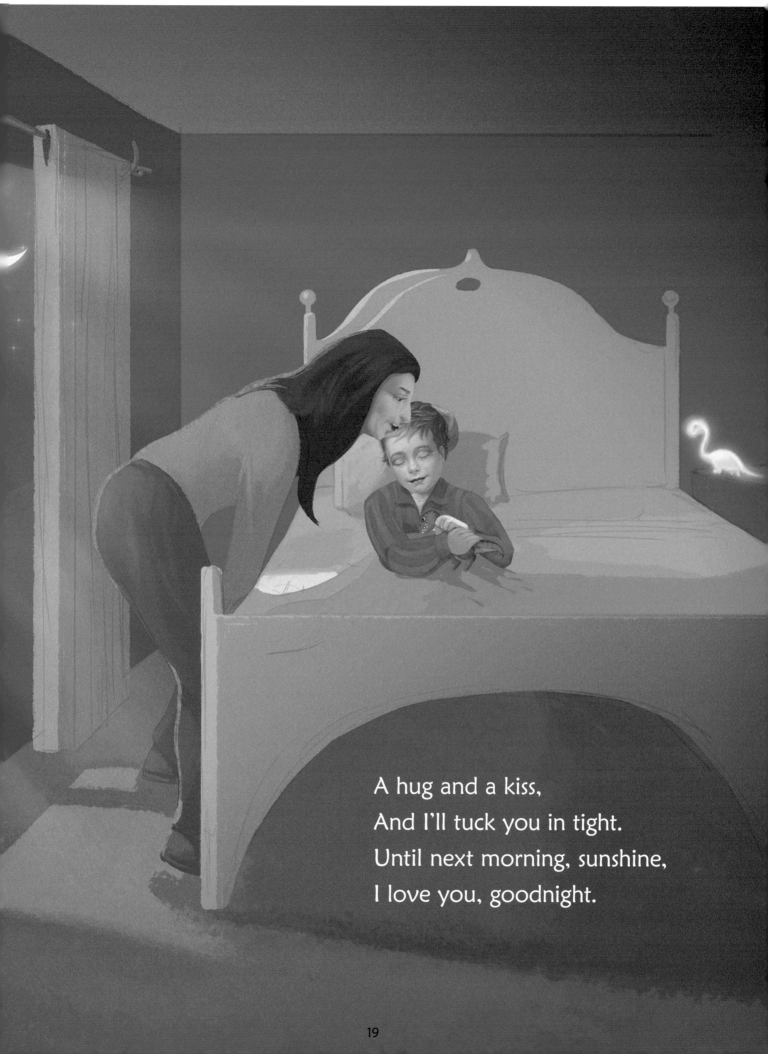

A hug and a kiss,
And I'll tuck you in tight.
Until next morning, sunshine,
I love you, goodnight.

The End

Printed in the United States
by Baker & Taylor Publisher Services